1

GARDENING

RAISING CHICKENS

BEEKEEPING

AND

MUCH MORE

(A FAMILY AFFAIR)

DEDICATED TO:

Joy Scott

And Mostly Written
From Her Wisdom

Thanks to all who helped with this project in any way.

TABLE OF CONTENTS

DISCLAIMER:

You know how when you read a how-to book, you always have a disclaimer. Here is ours.

This is a helpful "how to" book. We have included information about how to do a lot of things in it. You could write a whole book about just one subject area found in our book and a lot of people have. So there is a lot more information available out there. We have briefly covered each subject area. If you decide to do something found here, research and get all the information that you can and go from there. This book is a great place to start. It is also a compass to go by to make sure your future study is on the right track.

Here is the official disclaimer:

This book is presented solely for educational and entertainment purposes. The author and publisher are not offering it as legal or other professional services advice. While best efforts have been used in preparing this book, the author and publisher make no representations or warranties of any kind and assume no liabilities of any kind with respect to the accuracy or completeness of the contents and specifically disclaim any implied warranties of merchantability or fitness of use for a particular purpose. Neither the author nor the publisher shall be held liable or responsible to any person or entity with respect to any loss or incidental or consequential damages caused, or alleged to have been caused, directly or indirectly, by the information or programs contained herein. There is no warranty. This book is not intended as a substitute for the medical advice of physicians. The reader should regularly consult a physician in matters relating to his/her health and particularly with respect to any symptoms that may require diagnosis or medical attention. Always take safety precautions with whatever adventures you undertake.

CHAPTER 1
INTRODUCTION

This book started out with the purpose of saving and honoring the knowledge of Joy Scott (known in our family as our Mom, Grandma, and Great Grandma). Throughout our lives, our family has relied on her practical knowledge of so many different subjects. Every day, several generations of our family depend on this knowledge. The purpose of sharing this information is to preserve it for future generations -- those who may need to depend on this common sense and country way of life -- not only for life enjoyment, but perhaps for survival.

As we developed this book, we began to realize that not only our family, but also others, need the wisdom found here. More and more people are seeing the need to return to a basic, self-sufficient way of life. If you search through the internet and read books about country living, you find that people who are less than knowledgeable on certain subjects have written much. As our society has become more and more removed from this simplistic lifestyle, fewer people are really connected with it. The knowledge that is out there often is "really out there". Sometimes it doesn't even make sense. Thank God we are able to learn from our mother. She learned a lot from her own practical experience, but she also learned from her father, Bruce "Bill" Wells Young, and her mother, Virginia Blanche Kiser Young, as well as from her grandparents, Michael Washington Kiser, Amanda Clementine Pugh Kiser, Fielden Mack Young, and Caroline Alice Jones Young.

Mom hasn't been afraid to try anything. When it comes to having the knowledge, ability, and wisdom to do just about anything, she has outworked and out smarted many others. As we have talked to others about this book, we realize that there are many whose only way of learning about natural living is to rely on the internet and reference books. Unlike us, they don't have someone telling them, "Hey, that doesn't make any sense." They are flying blind and need practical advice. So, we have written this book to assemble knowledge of many areas so that we can remember this information, not only for the sake of the future generations of our family, but also to help others who want to learn. One day, this knowledge may even help people to survive and be happy and healthy.

We started with only gardening, canning, and freezing; bee keeping; and chicken raising. That has grown to include raising and using herbs, raising beef and milk cows, using deer meat, making maple syrup, and more. Others in our family have added their wisdom to Mom's to make this book.

This is a rich heritage of many generations and we are happy to be able to pass this on to you.

As in any book, it is good to always introduce the characters. The main character is Joy Scott. Joy has four daughters and they and their husbands came together to contribute to this book as well. I am Sandra Haga and my husband's name is Jim Haga. My other sisters with their husbands are: Debra Hawkins, and her husband Terry; Sue Combs and her husband Gwyn; and Joyce Henderlite, and her husband Doug. Also, thanks to Michael Henderlite, Joyce and Doug's son, for his contributions.

Mom,
You have given us all
much more than you could ever realize.
Thank you and we love you.

CHAPTER 2
GARDENING, CANNING, FREEZING, AND PRESERVING FOOD

Step 1. Plan the Garden

Winter is a good time to plan your garden. Think about what you want to plant, when you want to plant it, and where in your garden or property you want to plant it. Do what you can ahead of time so that when the time comes to get your plants and seeds in the ground, you can focus on that instead of planning. No matter what you are doing – bee keeping, gardening, or anything that is seasonal – it is good to use the off-season months to plan and get equipment, supplies, etc. together.

When planning your garden, decide how much space to put between the rows (how far apart you want the rows). Be sure to leave enough room between the rows for tilling. In order to do that, measure the width of your tiller. Most tillers have two sets of tines, an outer one and an inner. Take off the outside tines to be able to till between the rows. Measure the width of the inside tines to determine how far apart to put your rows. Be sure and allow extra space for bushy vegetables, such as beans and potatoes.

During the winter, you have determined what and how much you want to plant, so you should be ready to get your seeds and plants in the ground when the weather is warm enough to do so. Plant more of the things you love and will use more often. Also, remember that if you are saving seeds to plant in future years, you want to plant enough for what you use as well as enough to keep for seeds. Plant more of what you are going to preserve and less of what you cannot preserve. For example, if you want to can beans, plant more of them versus something like lettuce that you cannot preserve. You only need to plant enough lettuce to eat as you need it. Remember that you can plant some crops, like lettuce and spinach, in the spring and again in the fall. Whether you are trying to fit what you need in a certain space, or you are trying to determine how much garden to till, it is helpful to map your garden. If you are fitting your garden into a pre-designated space, you can determine how many rows you have room for after you have measured it. If you are fortunate and have unlimited space, measuring will give you a general idea of how much you want to plow. Remember that it is a good idea to keep hybrid vegetables away from non-hybrid vegetables.

Notes:

Sue added this note:

You might want to watch about planting things together that might cross-pollinate. I think only certain things can cross-pollinate. One example is I have always planted summer squash and butternut squash together with no problem. But I have had green peppers cross with jalapenos. I've read that tomatoes might cross pollinate but the way their blooms are made up, it is unlikely. I don't even know enough to scratch the surface of this topic, but it is more involved than we can cover here.

Step 2. Think About Seeds

About Heirloom and Hybrid

Hybrid seeds are seeds that have been genetically engineered. This process creates plants that are less susceptible to diseases, produce bigger vegetables, improve the color and yield, etc. These improvements are not always better. When plants and seeds have been genetically engineered, they do not have the same food value and taste as traditional vegetables and fruits. Also, one problem with hybrid seeds is since they have been altered, seeds saved from hybrid plants will not likely grow. If they do, they will probably produce inferior fruit. It is good to be able to save seeds from one year to the next as some people feel that seeds may become scarce as more people start to garden.

If seeds are not hybrid, they are called heirloom seeds. One thing to consider is if you get plants like cabbage, and tomatoes, etc. you can not always be certain if they are hybrid or heirloom. Many plants indicate if they are heirloom and if you do a little research you can generally find out. It is good to start as many things from seed as you can.

Places to get Heirloom Seeds

If you want to stick strictly with heirloom seeds, it is best to get them from a company that sells just heirloom seeds. If a company sells both heirloom and hybrid seeds, it seems they may not be as pure. Baker Creek Heirloom Seed Company is a good place to get heirloom seeds.

Notes:

Southern States provides a catalog which indicates which of their seeds are heirloom and which are hybrid. A key to this helpful information is near the front of the catalog.

Don't assume that all seeds/plants will be marked as to whether they are heirloom or hybrid. Some companies may not indicate this designation.

Seed Packets

Most seed packs contain good garden-planning information, such as how far apart to plant the rows, when to plant the seeds, and how much yield you will get from each pack. They indicate how many days until harvest; how deep to plant the seeds; the space needed between plants; preservation information (canning or freezing, etc.); how to start the seeds inside; and if you do start them inside, how to care for the plants. It also shows the best time to plant in certain areas of the country. This will help in planning and planting the garden. It is helpful to get seed packets that include this valuable information.

If you are planting herbs or flowers, the seed packs also tell whether or not these will come up again the following year, or if you have to replant them (more on annual and perennial to come).

Beware of seed packets that you can't see through. It may look like a good deal, but it might only have a few seeds in the pack. Checking the weight is a good way to compare the amount of contents.

Difference in Annual and Perennial

Annual plants only last one year. Perennial plants come up more than one year without having to replant. There are biennial plants too – like parsley. It grows from seed every other year, so after you have it planted for several years, you have a crop every year.

Notes:

Southern States Catalog
Sandra

Southern States provides a free catalog with their seeds, but you may have to ask for it. This catalog provides a great deal of helpful information, such as which seeds are hybrid and which are heirloom. It also shows the number of seeds needed for different family sizes and gives planting information about different seeds, including how far apart to plant and where, when, and how to plant. It is a good resource.

Step 3. Growing Plants

Sue and Gwyn

Starting Plants

The best way to ensure you have heirloom plants is to start your own. Tomatoes and peppers are good plants to start. Plant the seeds in the middle of March. Plants need a lot of light, so if you plant them too soon, they will get too tall and spindly due to lack of light (assuming you use no artificial light). If that happens, they are more difficult to transplant.

Save the black plastic containers you buy plants in to use the following year. These work much better than cardboard containers. If you don't have containers, Walmart sells one that is 18 boxes fastened together in a lid for easy carrying. This works good. You can also solicit your neighbors and family for their left-over containers. Plant three seeds in each cup. Only plant one seed in the Walmart cups as they are smaller. In the beginning, keep them wet with daily waterings using a spray water bottle. When leaves start to come up, reduce watering. Store the plant containers in lids from plastic tubs in order to easily transport them outside on warm sunny days. Remember that young plants are tender and will sunburn, so avoid full-strength sun until they are older. Since heat is important for seeds to germinate, using a heating pad will expedite germination. Once you see leaves, you can eliminate the pad.

Notes:

After the plants are about two inches tall, transplant them into cups and set them in tubs, not in the lids. To transplant them, use an ice cream stick to gently dig them out, making sure to get all the roots. Plant one or two in each small cup. You can use paper cups and it is best to cut the cups off a little over one-half of the way up. This works better than the plastic disposable cups, but if you have to use the plastic ones, put a drainage hole in the bottom. Be sure to include some of the dirt from the starter cups that came from around the plant roots. Water and cover with dirt. Be gentle. Don't become discouraged as they may not do well until they become acclimated to their new environment. This may take a few days. Keep fairly moist.

At times, the stems can be spindly and not very strong. Strengthen the stems by fanning them with your hand every day for several minutes. This simulates the wind blowing and the movement will strengthen them. Also, a lot of light is very important to help them be stronger.

Wait until after the threat of frost to put your plants in your garden, generally around May 10th for areas with climates similar to Southwest Virginia. When you plant them in the garden, pinch off the bottom leaves and cover that area with dirt. Plant deep but do not cover any leaves.

Step 4. Getting the Ground Ready To Plant

Plowing and Tilling

If this is the first time that the ground you are using for your garden has been plowed, you may have to disc it too. When you first plow it, it will have clods and sod with grass. Disking smoothes out the dirt and eliminates some of the clods of dirt. Any remaining clods, sod, and rocks need to be removed. Unfortunately, each time you plow, you will find more rocks that need to be removed.

Notes:

When to Plow

It is best if a garden can be plowed several months before planting. Snow puts nitrogen in the soil and old-timers often say "Let it snow on your garden after you plow it and it will help fertilize it." Don't plow when it is wet, or even damp, as it will cause clods and will be difficult to manage throughout the summer. To test, dig down about four inches to make sure it is dry underneath. If it is sticky enough to stick to your shoes, it is too wet. If you have access to chicken manure, spread it after you plow and before you disc or till.

It is best to till a garden several times before you plant then again right before you plant. You may have to till it several times to get good quality soil especially if it is the first time that the soil has been plowed. Later, you may not need to till as much. Also, till it when you need to control weeds; however, it is best to wait until the seeds are up so you don't till your seeds. Till until the vegetables spread into the rows so that you can't easily get a tiller through without damaging the plants.

Till the garden in the fall to eliminate weeds for the winter. It is best to pull weeds before tilling. It would be ideal to clean it off and plant a cover crop as erosion can occur without a cover crop.

Step 5. Fertilizing

You can buy fertilizer, but natural fertilizer like cow manure or chicken manure is better. Chicken manure is the best fertilizer, but it is powerful. Don't put on top of soil or directly on plants. It should be mixed with the shavings or straw from the chicken house.

Wood ashes are also a good fertilizer. Follow the directions in the previous step for adding fertilizer.

You can get a farm agent with USDA to test the PH of your garden to see what type of fertilizer, if any, is needed.

Notes:

Step 6. Choosing What To Plant

Sue and Gwyn

If you buy plants at a green house, they should be able to advise which ones are good for what use. For example, do you want a meaty tomato for canning or a good salad tomato?

Listed below are some varieties that are good (most of these are heirloom).

Note: Some of this information concerning dates and types of plants/seeds to plan for could vary with your location and the soil quality of your garden.

Peppers: *California Wonder*

Corn: *Honey Select* (good to freeze, just don't let it stay on the stalk too long).

Carrots: *Half Long Danvers* (good to cook – try cooking in the crock-pot and putting honey and brown sugar on them – delicious! When growing them, be sure to thin them. If you don't the growth may be stunted).

Tomatoes: *Bonnie Best* and *Rudgers*.

Beets: *Ruby Queen* – (Be sure to thin them.   You can leave them in the ground until a freeze).

Cucumbers: *Straight 8* or *Marketmore*

Summer Squash: *Straight Neck* (name of seed). These produce a lot of fruit so it is advisable to plant only a few. They need to be picked every day or every other day when they are small and tender.

Turnips: Sow turnip seeds in early spring for a summer harvest and mid to late summer for a fall harvest.

Butter Nut Squash: These, too, produce a lot of fruit so plant accordingly. They are similar to a pumpkin and stay on the vine until the end of summer.

Zucchini and Squash: Can be planted in the same row.

Notes:

Spinach: *Bloomsdale* - Plant early, around April 18.

Greens: *Rainbow Baby Greens*

Lettuce: *Mesclin* is a mix of different kinds. One kind is called spicy, and one is called mild. Sue prefers the mild.

Lettuce: *Red Wing Lettuce Mix* is good. *Oak Leaf Lettuce Mix* is not as good.

Plant Lettuce and greens around May 7.

Cabbage Plants: *Flat Dutch* - Plant May 7.

Broccoli and Cauliflower: Plants are better than seeds. The nursery can help with what kind, depending on your preference.

Peas: Plant early, around May 7. Leave in the ground after they have produced and they may reseed and come up again later.

Onions: Plant bulbs. There are different types of onions. Consider planting one kind that you can eat throughout the summer, one kind that stores well over the winter, and one kind that you use to can in spaghetti sauce, etc.

Helpful Note

Keep a diary of what you try each year and how it worked for you. Include types of seeds/plants you used, dates you planted, and what worked and what didn't work (example: late season, wet season, etc.). One idea is to use a calendar to record when you planted, when you harvested, quality of harvest, etc. Use the calendar as a guide to help you determine what and when you want to plant in following years.

Step 7. Planting

When to Plant

Wait to plant until after the threat of a hard frost. Each year will be different depending on the weather and your location. Generally it is after May 10th in Southwest Virginia and similar climates.

Notes:

Some things can be planted before the threat of frost is over, such as lettuce, spinach, peas, onions, broccoli, and cauliflower. Potatoes have been traditionally planted on Good Friday in Southwest Virginia.

Plant seeds and plants in the signs. Blum's Almanac is a good reference for planting according to the signs. This reference combines all aspects, including the moon phases and zodiac signs, and lists the best day of each month to plant above ground crops, root crops, flowers, seeds, etc. This is listed in the almanac under sections called "Gardening Guide", "Living By the Signs" and "Best Days" which is listed under each month. "The signs" are time periods that certain things do well if they are planted in those signs.

Fall and spring are both good times to plant carrots and beets. Mom says they do well in the garden after frost. When planting in the fall, plant them in time for the leaves and growth to come up before frost. Pull soil over any exposed roots for protection. They are protected by the soil and do good until a heavy freeze.

Barren Signs

Don't plant in Leo, Gemini, Virgo, Aquarius, Aries, or Sagittarius.

Laying Out the Rows

Straight rows make a garden look nice and make it easier to till. For straight rows, place a stake in the ground at each end of the row and run a piece of string between the stakes as a guide. Make sure each stake is the same distance from the previous row so rows will be straight. Mark your hoe at the ideal place and use it as a measure between rows. That way, you'll always have your measuring tool with you!

The seed packs usually tell how deep to trench the row for seeds. Make plant holes deep enough to cover the root and a good portion of the stem (to the bottom leaves). Always water plants and you can add Miracle Grow with the water if desired. Most seed packs indicate whether water is required at the time of planting.

Planting Root Crop Plants

Plant root crop plants in a deep hole and hill dirt around them.

Notes:

Step 8. Keeping Weeds, Bugs, and Pests Out of Your Garden

Bug Control

Mom doesn't use any kind of spray or bug killer. Lime (a more natural process) can be used on potatoes and probably other crops too. Southern States, or probably any farm store, has lime. Put it in a nylon hose and dust it on the plants by shaking the hose over them. Debra uses self-rising flour and that helps until it rains.

Important Note About Pesticides

If you have bees, don't use chemical pesticides.

Keeping the Weeds Out

Don't use Round Up or weed killer on or near your garden as these can be harmful to your health. There are natural ways to eliminate weeds. Put grass trimmings between the garden rows. This helps eliminate weeds, holds in moisture, and provides a natural fertilizer for the following year. Don't put this around potatoes as it can cause them to rot.

Sue and Gwyn

Sue and Gwyn limit weeds by putting three or four layers of newspapers down and covering them with dirt in between the rows. It is best to put down several layers of newspapers and cover them with a thick layer of grass clippings from yard mowings. Use as much grass as you have and if you do use grass, adding dirt is not necessary. This process must be done every year as the newspaper rots by the end of the season and it is usually gone by time to plow again.

Even if you use newspapers, you should hoe the plants periodically to keep the dirt around them broken up and soft. This also eliminates weeds. Don't hoe them until the plants are big enough to withstand the soil around them being disturbed. Be careful to disturb as little as possible.

Notes:

Keep in mind that when you add grass clippings to your garden, you may also be adding weed seeds. If you use enough layers of newspaper, the weeds won't get to the soil until the newspaper rots; so there won't be extra weeds during the summer. Some might come on during the next season.

Keeping Deer Out of Gardens

Sandra

To deter deer, Jim's mom and dad would collect hair from different salons and barber shops and sprinkle it around the garden, especially at the beginning of the season, to give off the scent of a human. Perfume can also be used with the hair. Our neighbors put a radio under a bucket and play it continuously. Don't use the radio until the garden is coming up so that they don't get used to it before the vegetables/plants are up enough for them to eat. Some people use fences or electric fences. One person was known to put peanut butter on the electric fence and when the deer sniffed the peanut butter, it shocked them. They would definitely stay out after that. We deter deer by using an electric device, like a dog whistle, that sets off a continuous ultrasonic sound that people can't hear. It seems to work pretty good. We tried one, though, that couldn't be set so that you hear it go off. That was a problem because it quit working and we didn't know it until the deer got in the garden. We are using one now that is set so that we can hear it go off, (it is set so that it only goes off at night when deer are out). It doesn't bother us, but if we had close neighbors, they might not love it.

Step 9. Canning

When to Can and Preserve Food

Can vegetables and make jellies and pickles during the last quarter of the moon. Refer to Blum's Almanac for more information on when to can.

Good Helpful Canning Guide

Ball publishes an excellent canning guide (Blue Book Guide to Canning and Freezing). It includes good instructions for canning, preserving, and freezing. The older versions may be better (around 1990), but be sure it addresses the kind of stove and canner you have. It can be ordered at www.amazon.com. Debra recently bought a new canner and the book that came with it is excellent.

Notes:

Gathering Jars and Lids to Prepare for Canning

Readying your jars and lids for canning is something that you can do in the winter so you have everything ready to can in the summer. Also, prices of canning supplies are less in the winter.

Lids and Jars:

After you plan your garden and decide what you are going to plant, decide what you are going to can. The number of cans you will need depends on how much you have planted and how well the crop does, but try to estimate how many you will need. You can use the older, sturdier glass mayonnaise jars as long as the lid size is the same as a canning jar lid and the ring "neck" is long enough for the ring to hold the lid or filler on firmly.

You can sometimes find jars at thrift stores and flea markets. Canvas your friends and family for extra jars. You will need to buy new lids each season as they cannot be reused. Your jar size (pint, quart, etc.) should be based on what you are canning and how much of that particular food you use at one time. If you are canning a large amount at one time, you may want to use two canners because the first canner has to cool before you can reuse it. The rings must stay on the jars for about 24 hours to secure a good seal. Because of this, you will need plenty of rings if you can on consecutive days.

It is not necessary, or even recommended, to store jars with rings as they can rust, making the jar difficult to open. Simply use the rings while canning, take them off the following day, and reuse them the next time you can. Be sure and wash them with warm soapy water and let them dry before storing them at the end of the season. If not, they will rust. You can't reuse the lids, just the rings.

Canning Process

There are different processes for canning: hot packing (the food is hot when put in the cans) and cold packing (the food is room temperature when put in the cans). The canning book will help you determine which method to use.

If you are hot packing food, the cans must be hot when you put the food in them. Wash the jars and put them and the lids in the oven at a low temperature (100 degrees) to warm them. Be careful not to get the jars too hot as they can break. You can also heat the can lids and rings in a pot of boiling water.

Notes:

Although it helps the taste and is recommended, vegetables don't necessarily require salt for safe food (except for sauerkraut and pickles). If you do use salt, do not use iodized salt as it can cause the food to darken or discolor. For healthier eating, use less salt than is directed. Fill the jars with vegetables, etc., then fill the jar with hot water if hot packing and cool water if cold packing. Avoid using boiling water in a cold jar as it could cause it to break. When filling a jar with food and water, leave about a 1 to 1 ½ inch head space.

Before placing the lids on the jar, wipe the lip of the jar. Food on the jar lip might prevent it from sealing. Make sure the jars are sealed tightly. Process time for each type of food is different so be sure and check your canning book.

Using Pressure Canners

The following directions are brief explanations. For more in depth details, see directions that come with the canner or the Ball Blue Book.

Avoid setting cans directly on the bottom of the canner as it can cause the cans to get too hot and break. Most canners come with a rack to use for this purpose. You can also use a canning rack that keeps the jars from touching each other. After jars are placed in the canner, put the canner lid on.

Put the canner on high heat until steam comes freely out of the vent for 10 minutes. This alleviates air trapped in the canner which can lower the temperature and pressure.

Close the vent by putting the jiggler on it and bring the pressure to the amount of pounds recommended for the food you are canning. Regulate the pressure by regulating the heat -- more heat makes more pressure. After it has heated and cooled for the time required by the recipe, take the canner off the heat and set where it can cool. It is important to let the pressure naturally reduce to 0 before removing the lid. Make sure no steam is coming out. Lift the cover, let it set for 10 minutes, then place the jars at least an inch apart on a cloth out of any draft. Don't touch the lids until the jars are completely cool and have set for approximately 24 hours. Remove the rings and label the food with a permanent marker on the lid (type of food and year it was canned). Store in a cool place.

Notes:

Dangers About Pressure Canners and Things To Watch For

Always watch the canner closely and ensure the pressure stays within the recommended pressure range. If it gets too high, the canner, your property, or you can be damaged/injured. If it gets too low, your food may be unsafe to eat. Make sure the gasket is placed correctly and that it is in proper working order (not dry-rotted or damaged). If it isn't, pressure will not build while canning. The lid will only close one way. Generally there are arrows to help you place the lid correctly. You can tell when it is closed properly.

Have your pressure cooker tested periodically. Your local Farm Bureau or Extension Office can provide this service.

The Ball Blue Book

The Ball Blue Book provides tips for using a pressure cooker and has directions for other types of food preservation, including freezing. It tells how many bushels of food will make how many jars of canned food and has a garden planning guide which shows how much food to plant for the yield you wish. It also has good information concerning the depth to plant seeds, the distance between rows, and other tips.

Removing Cans From Canner and Afterwards

Remove the jars from the canner one at a time and be careful not to tilt them. You can use jar lifters to lift the jars out of the canner, but be careful as they are not always trust worthy. Place the jars on a towel or rack (to keep them from breaking and/or damaging your countertop), away from a draft, and leave about an inch between the jars. Let the jars set undisturbed for approximately 24 hours.

During this time, do not tighten the rings or push on the center of the flat metal lid. The following day, you can test to make sure the jar has sealed by pressing the center of the lid. If it pops with each press, it is not sealed. Refrigerate and use as soon as possible. You cannot recan jars that did not seal.

Notes:

Date the Bags and Cans

When you are canning or freezing, always label (with a permanent marker) the jars and freezer bags with the name of the food and the date.

To Store Canner and Canning Supplies

Keep the jiggler, extra seal, and other supplies in a sealed baggie in the canner to keep them from being lost or damaged.

Wash rings after use and store them in a cool, dry place.

Step 10

Drying Seeds and Storing Them

The Grayson Beans and big October Beans that are in the Scott-Young family have been passed down for generations. It is important to save these heirloom seeds as they cannot be bought.

When harvesting these for seeds, leave some of the plants in the garden with seeds on them and allow them to dry on the vine if possible. Pick and hull them, then spread them out on an old screen, like Mom does, or a cookie sheet if you don't have a screen. Spread them thin so they get plenty of air circulation or they will mold. Don't let them get damp or wet and keep them in the sun and heat as much as possible.

Some plants "go to seed" after being left in the garden. Seeds will come out on top of the plants. Gather these seed for the following year. Some plants provide seed through their fruit (tomatoes) or vegetables (potatoes).

Freeze seeds or store in a dark, dry, and cool place. Storing in the freezer works great.

Notes:

Step 11.

Drying Fruits or Vegetables

Gran would thread fruits and vegetables on a thread and hang them up behind the wood stove. Make sure you store them where it is warm and dry. You can dry apples, green beans, and other fruit that way.

Drying Pintos

Let Pintos dry on the vine before picking and hulling them. Dry them on screens or baking sheets and either can, freeze, or just store in glass jars.

If you can dried pintos, soak them over night and rinse them the next morning. Boil them, put them in the cans and pressure can them.

Drying Onions

Tie onions in small bunches and hang them in a cool, dry area with good air circulation. Sue hangs hers individually as they seem to rot less. Plant and dig them in the signs so that they last longer when you dry them. If you want to store onions over the winter, it is best to plant the type of onions that are good for winter storage. Debra sometimes cuts and freezes hers. This works great!

Sandra

Jim's mom would string whole green beans and dry them. The long greener beans may work better than the Grayson beans. Use a big needle and run it through the center of the bean from front to back, not from side to side, or they will split in two. Don't hang them too close together on the string or the air won't circulate between them. Fry them whole in a frying pan or boil them in water. Old-timers call these "leather britches".

Notes:

Burying Vegetables in the Ground

Some vegetables can be buried in the ground to keep them fresher for longer periods of time. For example, Mom buries cabbages and has fresh cabbage as late as November, and sometimes later.

When burying root crops (carrots and beets), leave them in the ground and cover them with dirt for protection. If you are burying cabbage, dig a hole big enough to put the head in, place it upside down with the root sticking up, and cover it with dirt. Leave enough room between cabbages so you will have enough dirt for covering. You can cover all buried vegetables with straw to help hold in heat.

Storing Potatoes

Potatoes last longer in a dark, cool place – cool enough so they won't rot, but warm enough so they won't freeze (around 45 degrees). You can make a potato bin to store them in. Use wood instead of plastic for air circulation and use sacks to cover the potatoes for additional protection.

Step 12

Freezing Fruits and Vegetables

You can freeze many foods, including spinach and greens, fruit, dried pintos, peas, sugar snap peas, onions, peppers, and grapes. You can also stuff peppers and freeze them. Try to can and dry as many things as possible in order to save your freezer space for things that you can't or don't want to can, including meat.

Freezer burn is often a problem and it is caused by moisture and non-airtight packaging.

When you freeze food, be sure that it is as dry as possible before you put it in the freezer bag. Squeeze the air out before sealing the bag. You can buy sealers that vacuum pack foods. Be aware that some sealers don't vacuum pack foods, they just seal it without getting the air out which isn't helpful in this situation.

Notes:

Spinach, Greens, and Lettuce

Sue

Spinach, greens, and lettuce need to be picked while they are young and tender. Sue takes a butcher knife and cuts it instead of picking leaf by leaf. Scissors also work great. Wash it, use a Salad Slinger (Walmart) to spin it dry, then use a paper towel to further dry it. After it is completely dry, it can be stored in a zip lock bag in the salad crisper for up to a month

You can often harvest these types of greens several times before they stop growing.

Making Spaghetti Sauce

Debra

When you make spaghetti sauce, you can use Mrs. Wages spaghetti sauce mix. Blanch tomatoes by boiling them just enough so the skins start peeling. Peel and remove any bad places. Run through a blender and add the Mrs. Wages packet according to the directions on the back. You can also get Mrs. Wages salsa mix and a sweet pickle mix that you can use to make pickled beets. Sandra used Mrs. Wages Bread and Butter Pickle mix to make chow chow. For an extra zing, add some dill to it.

Pumpkin Muffins

We haven't added many recipes in this book as its main purpose was more than that, but pumpkin muffins is one of Mom's favorite recipes. She shares them with people in the neighborhood, people who need something special to cheer them up, and people who are sick or shut in. She likes this recipe because it is healthy, but sweet and good. Also, they are easy to take to people because they don't have icing which can be messy and they are great for freezing.

Notes:

PUMPKIN MUFFINS

4 eggs
2 cups sugar
1 16 ounce can of pumpkin
¾ cup vegetable oil
3 cups all purpose flour (Self rising is fine. If you use it, just use ½
                      teaspoon of salt, baking powder and soda)
2 teaspoons baking soda
2 teaspoons baking powder
1 teaspoon salt
1 tsp. Cinammon
2 cups (12 ounces) butterscotch chips

Beat together eggs, sugar, pumpkin, and oil. Comgine dry ingredients. Mix together with liquid mixture. Mix well and fold in chips. Fill greased or paper-lined muffin cups ¾ full and bake at 400 degrees for 19 minutes. Cool 5 minutes before removing. Yield about 24 standard size muffins.

Notes:

CHAPTER 3
CHICKENS

Raising Chickens, Caring For Them, Gathering Eggs, and Using Chickens For Food

Hatching Chicks

The best way to hatch eggs is under a "broody" hen. This is a hen that is getting ready to set on eggs in order to hatch them. This is called "setting". Chickens start setting on their own when they are ready. Sometimes you can encourage setting by putting wooden eggs in the nest. Strong chicks are usually the result when chickens start setting in the sign of cancer. Refer to Blum's Almanac for more information. It takes 21 days to hatch eggs.

If you can't encourage your hen to start setting, you can use an incubator to hatch eggs.

Care of Chicks

Most hatcheries only have chicks (day old) for sale in early spring. It is usually late enough so they don't die from cold exposure at delivery time. They are usually shipped one day and you get them the next day. Keep them inside a warm area when you first get them. Use a washtub for the first week or so until they are big enough to jump out. Put paper, shavings, or hay in the washtub to keep it dry and keep feed and water before them at all times. They will be messy and will get water everywhere. As they mature, they can be moved to a chicken house.

If you wait until later in the season, stores begin to run out of chicks. (Sandra: At the Galax Farm Supply, and maybe at other farm supplies, there is a chicken swap where people can swap older chickens that were hatched out earlier with younger chicks. This is good if you don't have the means to provide a safe, warm place for chicks.)

Notes:

Be careful when putting young chicks with older ones. If you don't do this correctly, the old chickens will peck the chicks to death. In order to survive, chickens have a natural instinct to be alert as to what is going on around them. Change can be considered a threat, including the introduction of other chickens, regardless of the age/size.

When you have baby chicks, don't put them with mature chickens at first. Mom has a small coop that she puts the baby chicks in when they have outgrown their washtub and she lets them out a little each day so that they can be with the older chickens while they are outside. When they are outside, they get along well because they are busy eating, pecking and scratching around. Eventually they will get used to each other. Watch them to be sure the mature chickens don't start pecking the chicks. Do this for several weeks before moving them permanently into the chicken house.

When Can I Expect Chickens to Lay and Set?

Mom gets her baby chicks in March and has always had Rhode Island Reds. They start laying eggs when they are around six months old. They will lay a while before they start setting, which is generally in the spring.

Debra

Debra's chicken house is made so she can gather eggs, feed, and water without entering the house. This helps if you have allergies. The waterer and feeder are next to the door and the nests (and eggs) are in a wooden box on the outside of the chicken house running the length of the house. The box can be accessed from the outside. There are eight nests and they are slanted thus the eggs roll so they can be easily gathered. She bought hers from an Amish business in Rural Retreat, VA.

Good Book

A good reference for chicken care is *Storey's Guide to Raising Chickens*, by Gail Dameron. It can be found at Tractor Supply.

Notes:

Putting Shavings and Straw On Floor Of Chicken House

Continual moisture on a wooden floor can cause rotting. Shavings and/or straw are good for soaking up manure and water. Scatter the shavings/straw lightly on the floor. You can get shavings free from lumberyards, wood working shops, and lumber mills or you can buy them at Southern States or other farm supply stores. If you accidentally get too much, just pull the excess over to the side in a corner and the chickens will scratch it out.

Some people put straw down in the winter because the chickens can snuggle down in it when the temperatures get very cold, especially if they have no light for heat in the chicken house. One winter we had below zero wind chill factors for several days. Some people had problems with their chickens and/or their combs and feet freezing. Putting down straw helps avoid this. Having a light for heat is better, but some people don't have electricity in their chicken houses.

When to Clean Your Chicken House

When shavings become soaked with water and manure, it is time to clean out the house or add more shavings. A chicken house needs to be thoroughly cleaned about once a year. If not, disease-causing organisms build up. Minimizing these organisms will help the flock stay healthy. Save the manure for the garden, herb garden, etc.

Winter Care

When it is cold, windy, and cloudy, Mom leaves a low watt electric light on for heat and light. Egg production drops off in winter months if you don't use a light. Don't do this too much, as it could be hard on the chickens. Some people carry warm water to them and they say this helps.

Mom lets her chickens out in the winter to eat as many fresh plants as they can find. They seem to really like the water cress she gives them out of the branch in the winter. She gives them handfuls of clover as long as it's available.

Notes:

Feed

Any farm store, like Southern States, can answer questions about which food to buy for what stage the chickens are in. Feed young chickens Starter Mash and when they start laying, feed them Laying Mash. The different kinds of food have different nutrients that they need for that time in their lives. Feed them cracked corn when they get bigger especially in winter.

Chickens thrive better when they are allowed to roam outside the house. When she can't let them out, Mom feeds them watercress and clover, which she believes causes them to lay more eggs. Egg production increases when they are given fresh live food and oyster shells help the shells to be harder. You can also feed them table scraps. You may not see a difference in the number of eggs, but it gets rid of unwanted table scraps. The frequency that you feed them depends on how old and how big they are. When they are smaller they eat a lot. You can tell if they are hungry by how they run to you when you feed them.

Keep feed before them at all times. However, if you put too much food out, they will start to mess in it and will waste it. You can buy feeders that prevent chickens from wasting their food.

Water

Chickens need to have access to fresh water at all times. Waterers come in many different styles. You'll want one that keeps the water clean and free of droppings, doesn't leak, provides enough water for the time period you need, and is easy to clean. For smaller chicks, you can use a quart or half-gallon jar with a special lid bought at a farm supply store. When the lid is screwed to the jar and inverted, water comes out as they use it. Larger metal watering containers are also available. The size you need depends on how many chickens you have and how often you can water them.

Notes:

Eggs

Gathering Eggs

Gather eggs three times a day, if possible, to avoid broken and dirty eggs. If they break an egg accidentally, they may start breaking and eating them. The more often you gather eggs, the more likely you are to avoid this.

Caring For Eggs

When an egg is first laid, it is wet, then quickly dries. This "wetness" is a film that helps protect against aging. Avoid washing the film off the egg as it won't stay as fresh as long. If there is manure or dirt on the egg, use a knife and scrape it off or use a damp cloth.

If you let an egg get cold in the refrigerator, don't take it out and let it get room temperature unless you are going to use it right away. It won't stay fresh. That is why Mom thinks that the ones you buy aren't as tasty.

Helping Chickens Lay Better

Production drops when chickens experience a change in routine, a change in people, or anything different or traumatic. Try to maintain a routine.

Mom hangs a strip of a sack in front of the laying boxes so they have more privacy when laying. She believes this helps them to lay better, as well as keeps other chickens from bothering them while they are laying.

Dusting Chickens for Lice

Chickens can get lice and this reduces egg production. Lice irritates a chicken causing them to break off or pull out their feathers. To de-louse, use a lice dust which can be bought at any farm store. Clean the house thoroughly to keep the lice from returning.

Notes:

It is sometimes difficult to distinguish between molting and lice. Molting occurs when shorter fall days signal chickens to renew their feathers to prepare for the colder weather. Because of changes in their body, they start to lose some feathers.

Meat Preparation

If you raise chickens for the eggs, the best time to kill them for meat preservation is when they have slowed down on egg production. One or two-year old chickens are better for canning than older chickens because they are more tender. Roosters are tougher than hens. After three or four years old, the chickens will be somewhat tough.

To Kill and Skin

We cut the heads off and put the chickens in a sack so they don't get loose and flop around without the head -- that isn't nice! ☺

Mom skins the chicken with all the feathers on it. She starts by cutting a slit along the back at the base of the neck. The fat comes off with the feathers and skin. Some cookbooks give directions on how to cut chickens for canning or freezing.

Cutting Up A Whole Chicken

After skinning and washing the chicken, cut the flesh between the legs and body. Bend legs in until you hear the hip joints snap. Slip a knife under the ends of the shoulder blades and cut to the wings. Avoid cutting into the body cavity. Put your hands in and pull the back and breast bone apart. Pull the wings off. Remove the guts. Be careful not to break the crop. It is like an extra stomach which holds food. It will be a mess if broken. Don't break the gall bladder because the gall will taint the meat. After cutting the chicken, rinse, dry, and freeze or can.

Sandra found a place on the internet to go for more details on all the steps and detailed pictures of each step. Go to butcherachicken.blogspot.com.

Notes:

CHAPTER 4
BEEKEEPING

Hive Care

In order to keep small animals from raiding a hive, keep it on something about two feet off the ground – just low enough in order to see into the top of the hive and work with it. Mom has hers on top of boards laid between cinderblocks that are stacked two high. Leave plenty of room between the hives.

Working With the Bees

When she is working with the bees, Mom wears two thick shirts, thick denim pants, and a beekeeper's hat. It is good to wear beekeeper gloves that come up to your elbows and are rubber at the hands so that you can work. Wear long tight thick socks that you can pull up over the legs of your pants and wear boots if you have them. Pull your pant legs over your boots and tie a heavy string around them. If you don't wear boots, make sure your socks are over your pant legs. You could wear two pairs of socks, and put one under your pant legs and one over your pant legs.

Smoker

A smoker is used to calm bees and is a necessity. To light the smoker, Mom puts strips of old rags in the smoker on top of paper and then lights the paper. Before beginning to work with bees, calm them with a couple of puffs of smoke. You can often tell their "mood" by listening to them and if they get rowdy and start buzzing a lot, smoke them again. Always have the smoker lit and ready. If they get out of hand, be prepared to give them a puff or two.

Notes:

Feeding the Bees

Mom says it is best not to feed the bees because they become dependent on this. Sandra said this, "I tried it and it is so true. When I first started, I fed two of my four hives because I felt they couldn't get out of the hive for weeks in the spring due to an unusually rainy season. At the end of the summer, the bees from the hives I didn't feed were working more than the bees from the other hives. When I stopped feeding the bees, they started eating the honey they had stored for winter and didn't go out and work like the others."

Sandra

Mites

Mites are small black bugs that can kill bees as well as get on larvae and kill them. To determine whether you have mites, insert a white "mite board" under the screen at the bottom of the hive. The board is white so you can easily see mites that fall onto it.

To get rid of mites, put a screen on the top super (or you can use a sifter). Sprinkle confectionary sugar on the screen and brush it into the screen. It will sprinkle down into the hive – you only need a coating. It doesn't have to go all the way through to the bottom because the bees will come up and carry it down with them. The sugar will coat the bees and they will start to clean it off one another. In doing so, they will eat the mites off one another. Do this every five days until the mites are gone. Check the mite board periodically and repeat as necessary. Don't do this on damp or humid days as the sugar will gum up.

You may need to treat the hive with something stronger if you can't get rid of them with the sugar. If you do, be careful and don't use anything that will kill the bees.

You can put a piece of soft peppermint candy in the top of the hive for the bees to eat. Once it is gone, add another one. Peppermint keeps away bugs so this will help keep the mites away. Once mites kill the bees, Mom's cousin Bob Young, who has kept bees for many years, says that the only way to be able to reuse the hives is to burn the inside of them with a torch.

Notes:

Storing Honey

Keep honey in the refrigerator if you aren't using it right away. It gets stiff, but keeps better. Honey is one of the few foods that doesn't spoil. If it gets old, it will crystallize and turn to sugar. If it does turn to sugar, you can heat it in the microwave just a few seconds and it will liquify.

Harvesting Honey

Mom uses the comb so when she puts the wax foundation in the frames, she does not use the foundation that has wires in it. That way she just cuts the comb and honey out around the edge of the frame. The honey should be capped over (cells are covered by wax) before it is harvested. Put the frame in a dishpan to cut the honey out. If you want to use the comb, cut it into sections, and put a section in each jar. Then fill the jar with honey and put a lid on it. Do not use heat to can it. The lid does not need to seal.

Separators are available that separate the comb from the honey by spinning it, but they are expensive. You can use a colander and a strainer if you want to separate it. After running it through the strainer, some people further strain it by running it through a pair of knee high panty hose.

Gathering Swarms

Bees usually swarm mid-day in the summer. You can tell if a swarm is ready to start a hive because they will begin to sound frantic -- they will produce a different, busier sound. Usually they will start balling up on the outside of the hive. They won't leave right away and they probably won't go very far at first. Watch and don't let them swarm and leave. Mom beats a metal dishpan with a spoon and the vibration causes them to land nearby.

Notes:

To Get the Swarm In The Hive

Often, bees will swarm in a tree and "ball up" on a limb. The queen will probably be in the center of the ball. Put a sheet under the limb and give them a couple of puffs of smoke. Put a hive body underneath it on a sheet. Tie a string onto the limb if it is a fairly big limb that could fall on the bees and hurt them. Cut the limb and lower it by the string down into the hive box. Make sure the queen goes into the hive box. They will love it and they will go in. Use the limb to gently sweep them into the hive. You can tell if the queen is there because all the bees will just flow into the box if she is there.

Bee Sting Ointment

A neighbor gave us a recipe for a homemade bee sting ointment that takes the "wallop" out of a sting. Keep it in your bee suit pocket and put it on as soon as you are stung. Just don't panic and come out of your bee suit to put it on. If you put it in a small spray bottle, you can spray it through your mask. You can also use baking soda or tobacco.

Home Made Bee Sting Ointment Recipe

1 cup clear household ammonia
1 teaspoon baking soda
1 teaspoon meat tenderizer

Sandra

Chilhowie Farm Bureau has a co-op store that has bee-keeping equipment at a good price. The hives are cut and ready to assemble.

Brushy Mountain Bee Farm's online store has bee supplies at fairly reasonable prices. You can access it at www.brushymountainbeefarm.com.

Our local high school agriculture department makes bee hives as a project to earn money for their program. They sell them at inexpensive prices.

Notes:

Buying, Building, and Storing Frames, Foundations, and Combs

A "super" is a large wooden box that holds frames. Supers stacked on each other make a hive. The bees lay their brood (eggs) and store the honey in these frames and they are one of the most expensive things you will need to buy. The ¾" wide wooden frames are the length of the super and contain bees wax foundation in them to entice the bees to add to the wax. Each frame and wax foundation costs about $1.50, but you will have 30 or more in each hive since each super has 8-10 frames and you can have 3 or more supers in each hive.

You can buy these already assembled, but most stores have them in pieces that will need to be assembled. To build, first use a utility knife to cut the small perforated piece off the bottom section. Use wood glue to glue the pieces together and, if desired, put a small nail at each corner for added security. At this point, add the wax foundation. There are two types of foundations: one has wires through it to help hold it in the frame and the other doesn't. Mom doesn't use the wire foundation because she likes to use the comb. When she cuts the comb out of the frames, the wires get in the way. If you use a separator to get the honey out of the frames, then you would need to use the foundation with wires.

When the frames are not in use, store them to reuse at a later time. Clean thoroughly before storing. Start the cleaning process by laying the frames out where the bees can find them -- they will clean the honey off in just a short period of time. Be sure to put them away from your hive as you can attract small animals and pests and can attract bees from other hives, which can entice them to rob your hives. Use a knife to scrape them, removing any old wax. If you store without cleaning, wax moths can lay eggs on them and when you put them in the hives, the eggs can hatch and destroy your hive. Papaw Scott and Sandra both had problems with wax moths destroying hives. A good way to ensure this doesn't happen is to put your frames in the freezer for three to five days before using them. You don't have to do this with new frames. Mom stores her frames in a large air tight zip up suitcase that nothing can get into to lay eggs. That works really well.

Notes:

If you don't use the comb, you can reuse the wax comb that the bees have built up in a frame for the next year. These can be stored in the freezer for several days in order to avoid wax moths. Be careful if you store outside the freezer, as the wax moths really love it. They have a way of searching it out.

Bees and God

Mom is an avid believer that God made the bees so they can take care of themselves. If you do a lot of things thinking you are helping them, you may be interfering with what they do naturally. For example, if you feed them, you make them rely on the food you give and that weakens them. The more you work with them, the more you interfere with their natural laws. In order to make them stronger, let them do what God created them to do naturally.

Taking care of bees (and all animals in her care) is something important to Mom. Animals are important because they provide for our health and welfare (honey, eggs, meat, milk, etc). For her, taking care of the animals is as important as the product they provide. Her adage is "Be good to them and they will be good to you!"

Benefits of Honey

We looked up benefits of honey on the internet and came up with the following benefits:
- Honey contains antioxidants which help reduce risk of some cancers and heart disease.
- Honey treatment helps disorders such as ulcers and bacterial gastrointestinal disorders.
- Honey helps increase athletic performance by maintaining glycogen levels.
- Honey reduces cough and throat problems.
- Honey improves eye sight, helps with weight loss, urinary tract disorders, bronchial asthma, upset stomach, and helps regulate blood sugar levels.
- Eating a tablespoon of honey a day from local bees will reduce allergies.

Notes:

Honey is one of the richest and purest natural foods with protein, carbohydrates, enzymes, minerals, Vitamins A, B1, B2, B3, B5, C, and biotine. It has anti-bacterial properties that are used in some cultures and in burn centers in the United States to prevent infection. It is naturally bacteria-free and does not spoil. Honey found in Egyptian Pharoah's tombs was still edible.

Bee Facts

Here are some interesting facts about bees. There can be around 30,000 bees in a single hive. A bee's life span in the winter is up to eight months; however, in the summer, it is six weeks because in the summer they literally work themselves to death. They keep the hive temperature a constant 90-95 degrees yearlong by producing heat through fanning their wings in the winter and cooling it in the summer by drawing in cool air.

Bees are very clean. The first job they do is to clean up the mess they make when they are born. They won't use the bathroom in the hive, sometimes holding it in for weeks at a time until they get sick if they can't go out during the winter. That is why honey is so clean.

Bees visit five million flowers to produce one pint of honey. Sixty percent of fruits and vegetables we rely on need honey bee pollination with an estimated value to United States agriculture of $14 billion annually. If all the bees died, it would only be a matter of a short while before we would die.

Places to Learn More

Sandra has found that one of the best books about Beekeeping is *Beekeeping for Dummies*. It is one of the books in the *Dummies* series. It is practical and written in a way that is understandable without being too technical. The facts above are from that book.

For videos on Youtube, search out Fat Bee Man. He has published many videos on different aspects of Bee keeping, showing how to do almost everything. He is an "old time" beekeeper who believes in doing things the easiest and most inexpensive way.

Notes:

CHAPTER 5
MAKING MAPLE SYRUP

Michael

There are more than a couple of reasons why homemade maple syrup is worth the effort. Like honey, it is an all-natural sweetener that is just as God made it without additives and refined sugar that can be bad for you. It is also a tradition that very few people continue and is a great thing to pass on to your children. Michael has been doing this for several years.

Tapping the Tree

When

Any kind of maple tree can be tapped to get sap to make maple syrup, but the Sugar Maple Tree is best because it has the most sap.

You want to tap the tree when the sap starts to rise (usually in February in Southwest Virginia). The specific time can vary due to weather. When the weather gets below freezing and heats into the upper 40's, the sap runs faster. The sap stops running on its own around the first of March, but again this will vary.

What You Need

You can buy a tap (the pipe you insert into the tree to get the sap) on Ebay. Instead of buying one, though, Michael uses a ½" PVC pipe cut into about 4" pieces. Grind off the end that goes into the tree so that it can seat in the tree securely.

You will need a portable drill (Michael uses an old-time brace and bit drill), a hammer, milk jugs, and twine to tie the jugs to the tree (Michael uses baler twine).

Notes:

Drill a hole in the tree a little larger than your PVC pipe. Insert the ground end into the tree (about 2" or 2 ½" into the tree) and tap it with a hammer until it is snug. Cut a hole in the side of a milk jug and run the tap into the hole. Take a piece of twine and tie the jug to the tree through the jug handle.

How Much How Fast

When the sap is running good, you can get five to six gallons of sap a day out of one tree so be sure and check the jugs frequently to avoid losing sap from overflow. (Michael is currently working on an idea to use bigger buckets instead of milk jugs.)

Making the Syrup

Michael uses his stove and an electric skillet to cook the sap into syrup. He starts with several pots, one on each eye, plus an electric skillet. At the end of the day he will cook the sap down to a gallon or so. That way he only has one pot to put in the refrigerator.

He cooks it on Medium heat at a temperature where it barely boils and where the bubbles are at the bottom of the pan with one occasionally coming to the top. If the temperature is too hot, it can burn and will have a bad taste.

Cook it around five or six hours, then put it in the refrigerator. Cook it again as you have time. When you can, put it in a smaller pot. Keep doing this until it gets thick. If it starts getting too thick too quick, turn the heat down. To see the real thickness, you have to put it in the refrigerator and let it cool because it thickens more when it is cold. If you get it too thick, add sap from a new batch. This is a trial and error process. Just keep working with it until you get it right.

Michael stores the sap in a five-gallon bucket outside until he cooks it down, then he stores what he has cooked in the refrigerator.

Michael is not sure how long the sap will keep until it sours. That's why he tries to cook it down everyday.

Notes:

When the syrup is to your desired consistency, pour the hot liquid in canning jars. You don't have to seal it like with fruits/vegetables, but if you pour it into the jar hot and screw on the ring, it will usually seal. Michael doesn't use new lids. You can use ones that have already been used.

How Much Syrup From How Much Sap

How much syrup you get will vary because of the sugar content in different saps. On the average, when you boil five to six gallons, you get roughly a pint of syrup.

Notes:

CHAPTER 6
HERBS

Planting Herbs

Although herbs can be planted at other times, it is best to plant them in the spring. Be sure to give them plenty of water when they are first planted.

Mint

Mint grows best where the dirt is moist (near a building, pond, creek, spring, etc.) and where it doesn't get evening sun. Mom doesn't water hers unless it wilts in the summer. You can plant it near a rock to keep the sun from drying the ground around it.

Catnip

Catnip grows best where it gets afternoon sun. Mint and catnip grow rapidly so plant it where it can be easily controlled. Also, plant it where it won't be mowed.

Both mint and catnip need to be pruned back to keep it from getting too long and scraggly. Just clip it and use it. You can give starts of it to other people but you must include the roots.

Dill

Keep it trimmed back or it will go to seed. You can transplant it.

Comfrey

Mom got hers from Gran and she has passed it along to several family members. Comfrey is good for a healthy heart and can easily be steeped for tea.

Notes:

Some other good herbs to plant:
Stevia
Parsley
Oregano
Rosemary
Chives

You can plant herbs in an herb garden, but that isn't necessary. You can plant them in pots or in window boxes and set them in a sheltered place during the winter. They most likely will come up the next year by themselves as long as they have not been exposed to extreme cold and are not annual plants. (Remember, annual plants have to be replanted each year).

Debra

Debra has an herb garden. Here are some of the herbs that she has planted:

Mint:
Peppermint (has a square stem)
Spearmint (is fuzzy)
Both are perennial (come up every year without replanting)

Comfrey: This herb gets big and has pretty flowers that the bees love. It can be used as a tea.

Garlic: You use the bulb of this herb and you also plant the bulb. Always leave some to come back the following year. You can get bulbs at any farm supply store, Lowe's, or even department stores.

Rosemary: This is a perennial herb.

Stevia: Stevia is an annual herb that is used as a sweetener. When drying, it's best not to use the stem as it does not dry as easily. However, when you use it fresh, it is fine to use the stem.

Chives: This is a perennial herb and has an onion flavor. You use the "leaves".

Oregano: Oregano is a perennial and is good to use in spaghetti sauce, soups, salads, Italian dishes, Mexican dishes, and many more.

Notes:

Basil: This is an annual herb and is good in spaghetti sauce as well.

Dill: Dill is a perennial and is great to put in fresh salads. Add it to cream cheese and pineapple for a dip or spread. Gran made dill beans with vinegar and dill – similar to dill pickles. You can leave the beans whole or break them.

You can plant some herbs in pots and hanging pots. It is good to put Mint in pots to keep it from spreading. Creeping Thyme is a good ground cover (moss-like) and looks pretty in pots. Debra has grown a variety of herbs, including Chocolate Mint, Pineapple Sage, and Lavender. Lavender is a perennial herb but is not as hardy as some herbs.

To Dry Herbs

Take the leaves off the stems and put on a paper towel or paper plate. Microwave on high for 30 seconds at a time until all the moisture is out. Make sure no moisture is left as it will mildew. Store in glass containers with lids.

Herbal Help for Sinuses-Debra

I was having six to eight sinus infections a year and the homeopathic doctor's office said antibiotics weaken your immune system. In January, 2013, I decided I would avoid antibiotics and it was a GREAT decision. I have not had a sinus infection in over a year. I have felt bad a couple of times, but used the lavender and it immediately took care of my symptoms. Mix a few drops of pure lavender oil with some olive oil and rub the mixture on your feet, especially on your toes. This is good for sinuses. Put pure Lavender oil on the tip of your nose to keep allergens away. I do this before mowing the lawn and sometimes when visiting crowded places.

Sandra

Swanson Vitamins have a good selection of herbs, vitamins, and natural health products. These aren't fresh herbs, but are bottled or liquid. Their phone number is 800-437-4148. You can find their website at www.swansonvitamins.com.

Notes:

Here is a sample of some herbs that Swanson sells (they have many more). I included this list to give you an idea of what some things are good for.

Beet Leaves	Natural source of carotenoids that can help prevent some forms of cancer
Birch Bark	Overall health
Back Cumin	Overall wellness
Burdock Root	Blood purifier
Catnip	Respiratory and stress reducer
Cayenne	Cardiovascular health
Celery Seeds	Liver and urinary tract health
Chamomile	Soothing and sleep
Cinnamon	Glucose
Clove	Gastrointestinal
Cranberry	Urinary tract health
Dill Seed	Soothes stomach
Echinachia	Builds immune system
Garlic	Cardiovascular and overall wellness
Horseradish	Urinary tract health
Kale	Nutritional Power House
Lemon Balm	Stress Releaser
Mint	Stomach soother
Onion	General health
Oregano	Overall health
Parsley	Fluid reducer
Rosemary	Free radical protection
Saffron	Overall health dating back to ancient times
Sage	Antioxidants
Sarsaparilla Root	Kidneys
Spearmint	Digestion and overall wellness
Spinach	Overall wellness
Stinging Nettle Root	Prostate
Thyme	Excellent for digestion
Turmeric	Liver and gastrointestinal
Wild Cherry Bark	Respiratory

As with any supplement use, take care when mixing with medicines.

Notes:

Don't use these herbs in their natural state unless you have learned to identify, prepare, and use them. This is just a good general list if you want to use these herbs from the herb store or Swansons. There are other companies that provide similar products.

Folk Remedies

High blood pressure: garlic
Headache: catnip or peppermint tea
Indigestion: catnip or peppermint tea
Anti cancer vegetable: broccoli
Heart: garlic

About Herbs and Vitamins In General

Mom believes in taking vitamins and herbs for certain ailments. She does caution that there are times when you need to be careful and not get "overloaded" by taking too much of a vitamin or herb. If you get too much of some vitamins/minerals, your body naturally eliminates them. But that is not the case with everything.

We have heard Mom say many times that it is more important to get the nutrients that you need for your body from eating the right kinds of food instead of eating anything you want and relying on vitamins to keep you healthy. It is better to eat right than to get your vitamins from a pill. The vitamins that you get from food are natural, just the way God made them for your body to use. If you have something wrong in your body, often there are foods that you can eat that have a healing property for that ailment. Research and find what would be good for you to eat to correct any ailments you may have.

Notes:

CHAPTER 7
OVERALL HEALTH

Mom comes from a long line of healthy people who worked hard and lived long. Her mother lived to be 93 years old and was healthy and of a sound mind until she died. Mom learned many of her health habits from her parents and they learned them from their parents. There are several reasons why Mom is as healthy as she is today. One, of course, is her serving God and having His peace in her life. She makes Bible reading and prayer part of her daily routine. Serving God is a focus in her life. Another reason is her genetic make-up that is probably like her mother's. Another reason is the life habits that she learned when growing up and that she continues today. It is this healthy way of life that we will talk about in this chapter.

Eating Habits

When Mom grew up, her family was self-sufficient. They grew their food, had cows for their own milk, and had their own chickens for eggs and food. Although they didn't eat a lot of meat at a meal, they had their own pork and beef. They did not eat many store bought or commercially canned foods but ate home-grown and home-preserved foods. They ate a well-balanced diet, something Mom continues to do each day. At each meal she tries to eat a dark green vegetable, a yellow vegetable, a fruit, and a little meat. They nearly always had some kind of beans for their meal. (Even today Mom loves beans and eats a lot of all different kinds.) They ate few fried foods and processed sugars and breads. Sweets consisted of preserves, molasses, and honey and breads consisted of cornbread, biscuits, and buckwheat pancakes (cooked on a wood stove which were delicious!). They drank milk at every meal because they had several milk cows that her father milked, at times selling the milk. They didn't drink coffee and only had soft drinks as special treats. They would drink grape juice and other home made juices. For breakfast they would eat a small amount of fried meat, biscuits, home-made gravy, and jam or applesauce. They would always eat a good breakfast, and Mom continues that today.

Notes:

As a family, they were very active and Mom maintains that active lifestyle today. She believes one of the keys to her good health is staying busy and working outside every day. She even has outside chores in the winter. The day before Sandra was writing this, Mom told her that she had trimmed five grapevines (in February). She had climbed the ladder to do them all and had to carry the ladder around to each grapevine. She works outside constantly and loves to work. She believes that this is a major key to her healthy long life and sound mind.

Mom doesn't go to the doctor much and tries not to take medicine. She says that it is easy to get into the habit of relying on doctors and medicine and that may cause many health problems of itself. It is better to rely on natural things in moderation.

Some Home Remedies

One old remedy Mom got from her parents is drinking one cup of water with one teaspoon of vinegar and one teaspoon of honey. She recommends doing this daily.

Benefits of vinegar and honey include: it self-detoxifies the body, is anti-aging, is naturally healing with naturally occurring antibiotics, and is an antiseptic which fights germs and bacteria. Vinegar has an alkaline forming ability to correct excessive acid levels in the body. It helps with arthritis, high blood pressure, and helps correct high cholesterol levels.

At one time, Mom had a lot of problems with her sinuses. She would start getting mucus in her nose which would then settle in her chest. She started doing something she had seen her grandmother do: rinsing her nose with salt water. She has not had many problems at all since starting this. She has felt better all over. She doesn't take any medicines now for sinus or colds because she hasn't needed any. She can get up in the morning and her head is clear.

To do this, she uses an eye cup or if you don't have one, you could just mix it in the palm of your hand. Mix two or three sprinkles of salt in warm water -- too much can cause irritation. Turn the cup up and rinse out both eyes. Then snuff this up both nostrils, one at a time, until you feel it going to the other side of your nose. Do this a couple of times. She believes it is important that you don't do this and go directly out into the cold.

Notes:

CHAPTER 8
FRUITS

Apple Trees

Trim apple trees in the spring before they get buds. This will help them produce better. Especially trim the long shoots that come up off the limbs.

Mom has grafted apple trees before. You can put one kind of apple on a different stem/root in order to have the sturdy root system of one type of apple that produces a good-tasting apple.

Grapevines

Trimming:

Refer to the almanac's zodiac and moon signs for specific days to trim grapevines in order for them to produce fruit and not produce growth. Prune just before the full of the moon in Scorpio or Cancer to discourage bugs and birds. (Joyce did this and she had a bird build a nest in the grapevine but it did not eat her grapes.) "Just before the full of the moon" means by the almanac sign and it doesn't mean that you have to do it at night or right before the moon comes up. In southwest Virginia, grapevines are generally trimmed in February.

To Transplant a Grapevine

Cut off a shoot from a vine and put it in water to root. Sometimes you'll find shoots coming up under a grapevine. If there are different types of grapes growing nearby, they might be pollinated by a different grape and be a mixture of the two types. Terry puts cottonseed on the ground around the grapevines and always has an abundant supply of Concord grapes.

If you plant a vine, you can have grapes in two to three years.

Check the almanac and plant them in the right signs.

Notes:

Grapes and Frost

If there is a late frost in the spring, you can cover the grapevine. Be sure to remove the cover before the sun comes up or it could scald the leaves. The heat of the sun on the frost is what damages the grapes.

Joyce and Michael

To Get Starts From Grapevines

Trim the vines in February (in the signs) and save the twigs if you want to start new plants. Cut the end closest to the trunk or ground at an angle and the other end straight across so you know which is the end you will put in the water (slanted end). Put them in water and put near a window where the cuttings will get plenty of sunlight. The starts will grow buds. Plant the starts in the spring in the signs and water the plants almost daily during the first summer.

Doug

Doug put a one-foot high mesh screen around the new cuttings to keep rabbits and other pests from eating the tender plants. To do this, drive three wooden stakes around the plant and wrap the screen around it. Attach it to the wooden stakes with nails or staples. It usually takes about three years for a vine to bear fruit. If you trim them correctly and take care of them, you can get up to 25 pounds of grapes off one vine in one year.

Trellis for Grapes To Grow On

When grapevines are big enough, build a trellis for them to grow across. If you are digging a hole for a post, be sure to put it far enough away from the vine so the roots won't be disturbed, but close enough so the vine can grow on it. It is best to dig the hole before you plant the vine. You can use two fence posts with a pipe across it. Mom has one grapevine tied on the side of the house with strings on nails (no trellis). Having it near the house protects it from frost and wind. Regardless of what you use to support your vines, make sure they are low enough for you to reach the grapes.

Notes:

Types of Grapes

Concord grapes are darker grapes and make pretty jellies. The old-timey pink grapes that Mom has are lighter colored and make good juice. Debra has white grapes that are her favorite for eating. She freezes them and uses them in shakes, teas, and just to eat.

Strawberries

Sue and Gwyn

There are two kinds of strawberry plants: June bearing and ever bearing. June bearing strawberries have strawberries in June, and ever bearing have strawberries throughout the summer. Sue and Gwyn believe it is best to plant June bearing so that you can harvest them all at one time instead of having them spread out getting just a few along throughout the summer.

When choosing the type of strawberry you want to plant, check for ones that are hearty over the winter and are good for the climate in which you live. This information should be available with the plants.

It is best to buy plants around the middle of April. You can order them from Gurney's seed company. At the printing of this book, they have 25 plants for $18. You can also find them at Lowe's, Walmart, or sometimes the local 4-H sells them. Always compare prices.

Replant every two years as they only produce for a couple of years. Keep in mind that they won't bear the year that you plant them.

For best results, keep them weeded. To keep weeds at bay put several layers of newspapers between the rows and cover them with a thick layer of grass clippings. If you don't have grass, cover the newspapers with dirt. You will have to do this every year as the newspapers rot by the end of the season and are usually gone by the time to plow again. This process keeps weeds down, moisture in, and rots to make compost. Keeping most of the weeds out of the patch will help the strawberry plants produce better. It is very difficult work but your results will be worth it. Once you weed the patch in the spring, check it once a week to avoid the weeds getting ahead of you. It is easier to weed when the soil is moist but be careful not to pack the soil down too much as that makes future weeding more difficult.

Notes:

Strawberry plants send out "runners" during the growing season as a means of propagating. These "baby" strawberry plants are connected to the mother plant by a root-like stem. You can either move the runners so they are in a row beside the mother plants or you can just let them be where they wind up. You can make freezer strawberry jam, canned jam, or you can freeze fresh strawberries. To freeze them, mash them with a potato masher. When you mash them, they are juicy so don't add water. You can freeze them in freezer bags.

Blackberries

Joyce

Blackberries ripen in late summer -- around the end of July or the first of August in Southwest Virginia. Blackberries vary in size and sweetness. Allow the berries to ripen until they are sweet and have a good flavor. Try eating a few of the berries before you pick. Sometimes they won't be as flavorful as at other times. The first berries of the season aren't as sweet as later berries, as they continue ripening for several weeks. Just keep checking until they have a good taste.

One year we picked the berries too early and they weren't very sweet. A lot of rain may cause berries to be tart, but when canned with sugar water syrup, the blackberries taste fine.

Easy Picking Style

Instead of picking one berry at a time and putting each one separately in the bucket, pick one at a time and hold them in your hand until your hand is full. Then put the whole handful in the bucket at one time.

Preparing Berries

Wash and check the berries twice for debris and bugs. Drain well in the colander.

Notes:

Canning Blackberries

Pack the berries loosely in cans leaving a ½ inch headspace at the top of the can.

The Ball Book has recipes to make syrup. Joyce uses a light syrup. Pour it over the berries in the can and put lids on. Follow the recipe directions.

Light Syrup Recipe

Combine 2 cups of sugar and 1 quart of water. Stir until the sugar dissolves. Makes 5 cups of syrup.

Process pints 15 minutes and quarts for 20 minutes in a hot water bath. Hot water bath means boiling them in a regular canner, not a pressure cooker.

When you take the cans out of the hot water bath after processing, set them on towels to cool. Leave them for a day without taking the rims off or pressing the lids. Remove the rings after 24 hours. You may have to wipe cans as they may be sticky.

To Freeze

Water and non-airtight packaging contributes to freezer burn so drain the berries, let them dry thoroughly, and freeze them in airtight packaging.

Date the Bags and Cans

Label freezer bags and cans with a permanent marker. Include the contents and date.

Notes:

Joyce's Favorite Blackberry Cobbler Recipe
(Isn't really sweet)

Mix 1 cup sugar, 1 cup flour, and 2 teaspoons Cinnamon in a bowl. Add 1 cup milk. Batter will be runny. Melt a little less than ½ stick of butter in a 9" x 9" pan. Pour in mixture and carefully spoon 1 quart of drained berries on top. Bake 350 degrees for 45 minutes. (Double this for a 9 X 13 pan.) Joyce acquired this recipe from one of her good friends, Janet Breen.

Places To Find Fresh Inexpensive Fruit

Sandra

If you don't have your own fruit trees, you can get inexpensive fruit at orchards. For example, the apple orchards in our area sell second grade apples for 1/3 the price of their Grade A apples. These are called "deer apples" because people buy them to feed their deer. They are just a little smaller, and may have a few spots, but they are good apples. You can probably get the same deal for other types of fruit like peaches, etc.

In some orchards and strawberry fields, you can save by picking your own.

Another place to find good bargains is with local farmers. For example, in our area there are a lot of pumpkin farmers. They can only sell the Number One grade of pumpkins. Often they use the others to feed to cattle, but sometimes many of them rot in the field. They will often give them to you if you ask and if you pick them. You just have to ask at the right time -- after they harvest them and before they begin to rot in the field.

Gleaning

Just like in Bible times, people still glean today. There are some farmers in our area that let people get what is left over in the field after the harvest. Sometimes companies harvest with machines, and there is a lot left over in the field. Instead of letting produce rot in the field, they will let you pick what is left. Some may charge, but many of them offer this at no cost.

Notes:

CHAPTER 9
DEER MEAT

Cooking Deer Meat Steaks and Roasts in the Crock Pot

Sandra

Most people use recipes but you know me, I do it the easy way. Easy may not always be better! Our deer meat is vacuum sealed by a meat processing company. The wild taste of deer meat is in the blood and the amount of wild meat taste depends on how it is processed and whether or not the blood has been properly drained.

I put the meat in hot water to thaw it. Don't put it in the microwave to thaw as it doesn't give the blood time to drain out of the meat. It is important that it thaws completely so that the blood runs out into the bottom of the bag. When it is fully thawed, put the meat in water and let it set until you no longer see blood (about five minutes). Some people let it set over night but I just let it soak for a little while. Some people soak it in vinegar, or other marinades, but I don't. After it soaks, take it out of the water. If I am going to cook it in the crock pot, I baste it with a lot of thick steak sauce and put salt and a lot of pepper on it. I let it set in the crock pot with the sauce, salt, and pepper for about 10 minutes before I add water. Add enough water to cover the meat. Onions also add a nice flavor and you can use as many as you want. Cook overnight and add potatoes and carrots a couple of hours before you are ready to eat. If I put the carrots and potatoes in right before church, they are good by the time we eat. That is a great meal to fix on Sunday mornings. I do this with both the roasts and the steaks. The steaks cook all to pieces but we like it that way.

Frying

Thaw the meat the same way as described above. Turn the eye on fairly high and brown the meat on both sides, then turn it on low. Cook until done then add steak sauce on both sides. Simmer until tender – about 20 minutes. Adding onions makes it tasty and helps reduce the wild taste.

Notes:

Jerky

There are many different jerky recipes, but I use an easy recipe. I use steak sauce and steaks, but you could use tenderloin. I use steaks as the pieces are larger than most tenderloin. Thaw the steaks keeping them soft enough to cut but frozen enough to cut easily. Slice them in ½ inch strips about five inches long and three inches wide using a meat slicer (or a knife if you don't have a slicer). If you slice them too thin, the meat dries out making it hard. Rinse the meat until the water runs clear and all the blood is gone.

Soak them in steak sauce and put them in a dehydrator with onion salt and a lot of pepper. I have read on the internet that you can dry them in the oven, but I haven't done that. It would probably work good though.

The amount of time you dry them depends on your dryer, the thickness of the meat, and your preference. If you like jerky harder or chewier, adjust the drying time to what you like. If you leave them too long, they will get so hard that they are difficult to chew. I used to dry them overnight, but they got too hard so now only dry them for several hours. Be sure that they dry enough as you do not want pink or raw-looking meat. The thicker the pieces of meat, the longer you need to dry them. If they get too hard, then don't leave them that long the next time.

Store them either in jars with lids or plastic zip lock bags. Softer jerky can be frozen or stored in the refrigerator.

Notes:

CHAPTER 10
RAISING CATTLE FOR YOUR OWN MEAT

Beef Cattle-Raising a Steer For Your Own Beef

Michael (With Some Added From Terry)

It is better to buy your calves from someone you know as the calves will likely be healthier. If you can't, however, you can always buy the calves at the cattle market. If you get a calf from the market, they may have a hormone implant. Michael says that he never gives his beef a hormone implant, and there is really no way to check if someone else has.

Once you get your calves, vaccinate and de-worm them. You can inject the calves yourself and can get the medicine from Southern States or at the cattle market. If you purchase at Southern States, you can buy in either 10 or 50 dose packages. If you get the calf from the market, you can get single doses there.

When raising cattle, make sure they always have plenty of grass and water. You need to start grain feeding them for about 60 days before slaughtering. Start with a 5 gallon bucket 1/3 full and gradually increase it once a week. While grain feeding cattle, they can gain more than four pounds a day. It puts marble (some fat) in the meat, but not too much. Keep water in front of them at all times.

Slaughtering and Packaging

Mom takes her beef to:
Russell Meat Packing
Phone: 276-794-7600 or 877-820-2418
Address: 315 Sulfur Springs Circle, Castlewood, VA 24224
It's important to call several months in advance as they are very busy.

Debra takes her beef to:

Williams Meat Processing
Phone: 276-686-4325
Address: 3823 Old Stage Road, Wytheville, VA 24382

They generally have their beef slaughtered in November and make the appointment no later than August.

Notes:

Regardless of where you take it, make sure they vacuum pack the meat.

From our experience, the yield of edible meat from a beef is about ½ of the live weight of the steer. This depends on the breed of steer you have. If the steer is 1,200 pounds, you will get around 600 pounds of meat.

Cost Comparison

Based on our family experience, it is more economical to raise steers for beef than to buy beef. Another added benefit we notice is the superior taste and the lack of hormones, antibiotics, and other unwanted chemicals. When calculating the cost efficiency, we considered the cost of the steer; the feed; and the hauling, slaughtering, and meat processing fees.

Having a Milk Cow and Raising Calves

Raising a cow provides many benefits, such as providing fresh milk, cream, butter, cottage cheese, and yogurt. Holsteins are good milk cows. It is best to get a cow from someone you know or get it as a calf and raise it.

After the cow has her first calf, she starts producing milk. You generally have a cow bred every year. About eight months after she has her calf you would breed her again. Stop milking her about 30 to 45 days before she has her calf so she will produce colostrum.

Colostrum is special milk that cows have for their calves. It is thick and yellow with a lot of nutrients. If she has more than is needed, it can be frozen and saved in the event a future cow can't feed her calf or it can be sold. Michael gives it away if someone needs it for their calves. It is crucial that newborns have colostrum for the first 24 hours as they will die without it. You can start drinking the milk again when the colostrum completely clears. Several days after the calf is born, you will be able to tell when the colostrum is gone because the milk looks normal.

It is good to note that if you stop milking a cow, it will eventually cause her to go dry (not produce milk). A cow never goes dry on her own. She will continue to produce milk unless you stop milking her.

Notes:

Sometimes a young, inexperienced cow will reject a calf and not let him suck milk. If you encourage the mother, sometimes she will go ahead and let the calf eat. You can tie her back legs together so she can't kick, put her in a "head gate" (gate used to hold cattle for medical treatment), and force her to let the calf suck. It may take several days of doing this before she lets the calf suck.

Bottle Feeding

If the cow won't let the calf suck, you will have to bottle feed the calf. It is imperative that they get colostrum and you can get this at any farm store. You can also buy the bottles at a farm store. Sometimes, for convenience, you might want to wean the calf while it still needs milk as it is easier to mix milk in a bucket and give to the calf rather than to bottle feed. To make this transition, let them suck on your thumb covered with milk, then put your thumb in a container while they are sucking on it. It may take a few days before they drink on their own.

Preparing Milk for Use

After milking the cow, strain the milk to remove any dirt. Use a cloth that is somewhat porous (like a cheesecloth) as a strainer. After you strain it, let it set in the refrigerator until the cream rises to the top. If it sets until the cream rises before it is strained, that is fine. Shake it, then strain it. The cream will rise to the top again. It takes a while for the cream to gather to the top, but you'll know when it is complete. After the cream rises to the top, skim off the cream. Cream can be used for making butter or for cooking.

Churning Butter

To churn butter, use whole milk that is from a dairy or from your cow. Whole milk means that the cream has not been separated from the milk. You can't use store-bought milk that has been pasteurized because that mixes the cream with the milk. Use the cream skimmed off the top of the milk to churn into butter. You may need to save the cream off several "milkings" to be able to have enough to churn. Let it set out of the refrigerator a few days -- just long enough for it to start to sour.

Notes:

114

You can churn butter in several ways: by using a churn, shaking the cream in a jar, or Sandra read on the internet that people use a blender, or a food processor. It only takes about 15 minutes or so. When you see the butter forming, turn it, shake it, or blend it slower, whichever you are doing. This will gather the butter together. Take the butter out of the milk. Wash it in cold water to get the buttermilk out so it isn't so sour or sharp. "Kneed" it to get all the liquid out and salt it to taste. Put it in a butter mold to shape it or you can pat it together or put it in any type of container. Refrigerate it. Use the buttermilk to drink or to make biscuits. Several recipes use buttermilk. If the butter or the buttermilk gets too old it will get strong.

Other Things To Do With Fresh Cow Milk

You can also make cottage cheese, different kinds of cheese, and yogurt. You can find recipes and directions of how to do these online.

How Long Will Milk Last?

Store-bought milk that has been pasteurized will last longer than fresh milk. The process it goes through causes it to last longer and it may last a while before it sours. Keep in mind that fresh milk hasn't been through that process so won't last nearly as long.

Notes:

CHAPTER 11
SIGNS

The Blum's Almanac has great information on how to use the signs for daily living. Look up both the zodiac and the moon signs. It may give a couple of choices for planting signs, etc. The first sign shown is the best sign to use.

Planting and Harvesting Signs

- Planting is best done in the signs: Scorpio, Pisces, Taurus, or Cancer.

- Plant things that yield above ground crops in increase of the moon. Plant things that yield below ground crops when moon is decreasing.

- Never plant anything in the barren signs.

- Pick apples and pears during the old moon and bruised spots will dry up. If picked in the new moon the spots will rot.

- Harvest all crops when the moon is growing old. They keep better longer.

- Dig root crops for seed during the Third Quarter of the moon. They will keep longer and they are usually dryer and better.

- Grain intended for seed should be harvested at the increase of the moon.

- Can vegetables, make jelly and pickles during the last quarter of the moon.

Timber and Fence Posts

- Cut timber in the waning of the moon. It will dry better.

- Set fence posts when the moon is growing old to prevent them from working loose.

Notes:

Weather Sayings

Weather saying: The number of winter snows can be told by counting the morning fogs in August.

When katydids begin singing in the fall, it will be 40 days until frost.

Some Signs of a Rough Winter

If wooly worm is black on front, there will be early cold and early winter weather. If it is black all over, it will be a bad winter throughout.

If squirrel tails are bushy and they begin to gather nuts early in September, the winter will be bad.

If hornet nests are built high, there will be a low depth of snow.

If corn shucks are thick, the winter will be bad.

A little poem helps us to remember about onionskins:

Onionskins very thin
A mild winter's coming in.
Onionskins very tough
Mean winter's coming cold and rough

Tree bark thickness is another mountain folklore of winter.

The Bible Mentions Signs

The Bible mentions signs for weather. In Matthew 16:2-3 Jesus told Pharisees, "When it is evening ye say, It will be fair weather: for the sky is red. And in the morning It will be foul weather today: for the sky is red and lowering...

McGuffeys Reader (one of the readers used for many years in early schools) says it this way. "Red clouds in the morning, sailors take warning. Red clouds at night, shepherd's delight." Mom learned this saying when she was a small child.

Notes:

120

CHAPTER 12
ELIMINATING PESTS/TANNING SHEEPSKIN

Getting Rid of Skunks, Possums, and Raccoons

Mom captures these pests in a long rectangular cage that traps living animals. You can buy these. She has Gwyn discard the skunks!

Gwyn

Be very careful when sneaking up on a skunk in a trap. Go behind them and cover them with a tarp so they can't see. They aren't likely to spray you if they are covered so keep them covered while you are working with them. Put them in your vehicle and take them several miles from where you caught them. If you don't take them several miles away, they could come back. Traps have a wire on the door so that you can pull the wire and the door will open. Hold the edge of the tarp over their head while you open the trap. Flip them out so that you more or less throw them out from you. They are more interested in getting away than trying to get back at you.

You can do this instead of shooting them and taking a chance of them spraying around your house.

To Make a Sheepskin Mat

These directions tell how to make a sheepskin mat. They were handwritten in Mom's mother's handwriting.

To Prepare Sheepskin to Make Mats

Wash the fresh skin with a strong lather of soap and hot water. Allow it to stand until cold. Squeeze and rub the wool until it looks clean and white, then carefully rinse all the soap out of it.

In two gallons of hot water, dissolve one pound of salt and one pound of alum, and soak the skin in it for 12 hours. Hang it up and let it drain thoroughly, then stretch it carefully on a board to dry. *Continued.*

121

Notes:

Stretch it several times while drying. Before quite dry, sprinkle over it on the flesh side: one ounce each of finely pulverized alum, and saltpeter. Rub it in well, then try the wool to see if it is firm to the skin. If not, let it remain a day or two then rub over again with alum. Fold the flesh sides together. Hang in the shade for two or three days, turning them over every day until quite dry. Then scrape the flesh side with a blunt knife, and rub it with pumice.

HELPFUL HINTS

Fixing a Rusty Cast Iron Pan:

Put it in a hot fire and burn it inside and out. Take it out and put vegetable oil in it and season it in the oven in low heat.

Notes:

TRIBUTE TO OUR MOM

When we realized that there were a lot of people outside our family who were interested in this book, I thought about just adding this section to a particular version that would be just for our family. I decided not to do this for a couple of reasons. The main one, we wanted to honor our Mom before everyone, not just before our family, because she is that special. Another reason I decided to leave this is that through these pages I hope that Moms everywhere are encouraged. I hope you see the importance of your role as a mother and that you realize you are working on a legacy of your own. If you are a Mom, you probably will one day have grandchildren, great grandchildren, great great grandchildren, and on from there. Most of them you may never know. What kind of legacy are you leaving them? I pray that through these pages you can find hints that will help you to become a better Mom as you work on this legacy of your own.

MOM,
THIS CHAPTER IS YOURS. WE WANTED TO TAKE TIME TO TELL YOU HOW MUCH YOU MEAN TO US. FROM YOUR GIRLS.

A MOTHER OF JOY
REBA "JOY" YOUNG GENTRY SCOTT
FROM: DEBRA

Joy ... what an appropriate description of the woman God chose to be my mother. Little did her parents know how much joy she would bring to others when they named her. When I think about the joy my mother shared with me as a child, I remember family picnics, trips to the barn to play on the hay, routine chores like mowing the yard and canning (which our parents taught us to enjoy), learning tree identification, laughing around the supper table, quilting, going to the dip dog stand, praying as a family, singing and playing guitars at family reunions, collecting leaves, participating in Girl Scout outings, going on camping trips, reading on a rock in the middle of New River, experiencing Bible School, and cleaning house and reading to elderly neighbors. These are just a few cherished memories of my childhood. The one common denominator with all these activities was my Mother. She had a way of teaching us valuable lessons and all along, we thought we were just having fun! She had a remarkable way of changing jobs to joys.

Mother always completed our family and she still does. When I have a particularly challenging day or am discouraged, she is the person I go to. She is my defender, my biggest supporter, my therapist, my inspiration, my teacher, and my coach. She has helped me work through many things in my life and has taught me (and is still teaching me) so much. I can pass the skills she has shown me to my children and they, no doubt, will pass them along to their children. Her legacy will be long-lived. What a wonderful gift to pass on to those you love. Her wisdom will flourish for generations to come.

She taught me how to work through trials and tribulations with confidence, dignity, poise, and an unwavering trust in God. She taught me to rely on God for daily guidance, to pray, and to love God with a steadfast love. She is a woman of God and has taught her daughters to be the same. She taught me to embrace thankless selflessness by always putting her needs and wants aside for her family, church, community, and God. She taught me to love others for who they are and not for what they look like or where they have been in their lives. She taught me to love and respect the land and to be a good steward of the material blessings God has chosen to give me. She taught me to cherish the little things in life, like a hummingbird or a wildflower blossom. Through her actions, she taught me how to nurture my children with a deep sacrificial love. She taught me to work hard, be patient and diligent, and to be a good example to others. And last, but not least, by consistently bringing our family together, she has taught me the importance of strong familial relationships, which is something our family will cherish for years.

She's been there every step of my life, from childhood to teenage years, to young adult years when I had young children of my own. And even now, when my children are grown and gone from home, I cherish our conversations and time together. Her wisdom and insight are endless. She seems to always know what to say to help me through a trial. As I age, she has become my best friend. How do you begin to tell, in a few short paragraphs, how much someone means to you that has molded you and made you into the person you are? How do you attempt to describe the joy you feel when you reflect on all they have done for you? It's impossible and this humble and feeble attempt doesn't seem worthy.

Words cannot describe how much my mother means to me. I thank her for all she has done and is still doing. I love her with all my heart … and then some!

FROM JOYCE

When Sandy, my sister, asked me to write a tribute to our Mother for her book, I was overwhelmed. Where do I start? Momma has always been there for us. She didn't work outside the home except during short periods of substitute teaching at the school. She molded us physically, mentally, academically, and spiritually into the people we are today.

Physically, she always stressed taking care of ourselves and striving for general good health. She promoted activities that kept us busy. If nothing else but telling us to go out and run around the house ten times when we were bored! She also encouraged and taught us healthy eating habits. She canned most of our food. We had fresh beef and chicken from the farm, eliminating preservatives from our bodies through the years.

Mentally and academically she challenged us to be the best we could be in whatever endeavor we chose to participate in, whether it was learning all we could at school or studying for tests. I've heard her say more than once that she wanted us to be well-rounded individuals. She supported us in a variety of activities and helped with many of these activities....Bible school, scouting (she was my Girl Scout leader for many years), basketball, and especially our music. I once remember at one of the many music recitals I could only remember the first page of a three page piece of music. I just kept playing that first page repeatedly, hoping the rest of it would come to me; it didn't so I just finished the selection with a chord. No one probably ever knew the true story behind that goof but Mom, my music teacher (Janet King), and me. Momma and Miss King never mentioned my mistake and praised me for doing a nice job. Then when we started becoming leaders, as young adults and adults, she encouraged us to take leadership roles in our church and community.

Spiritually, there was never a day that went by that God was not lifted up in our family. There were struggles, as with any family, but never anything that Momma and Daddy with confidence in God didn't overcome. As small children we were taught to say grace at the table and nightly prayers. Mother knew we were not perfect and was always willing to forgive and forget and start over. Thank goodness for that! The values and characteristics she taught and instilled in her children were based on biblical values. The faith she passed on and instilled in us was part of her heritage from her parents and I am so very thankful for that legacy. This legacy is the most important goal that I want to pass on to my son, Michael.

All children, who are fortunate enough to have been brought up in Christian families, probably think they have the best Mom in the world and that's how I feel. I am so thankful and blessed for the many things she did and still does for her family; how she is always there, is willing to listen, still answers questions when we seek information, or has insight to tell us how to handle specific situations. Proverbs 31:10-31 describes my Mother and it is with all sincerity that I can say "Her children arise up, and call her blessed..."

MEMORIES
FROM SUE

LETTER TO MOM

I have learned so many things from your example and the way you lived your life while we were growing up. Some of my favorite memories help me see how you influenced me to become who I am today. These are the kind of memories that give you that warm, fuzzy feeling.

I remember sitting in the hammock in the back yard playing with kittens. I remember riding to and from Sugar Grove in the summer with the windows down. I think most of these trips were to take the trash off. I was stung by a wasp on one of these trips, which wasn't too warm and fuzzy; but there are always those stinging memories too. The smell of mint still takes me back to days spent playing in the creek, the water was so cold that our feet would be numb. We would step out for a minute and get right back in to see how far we could get. We just enjoyed life as it came. We didn't have to be doing anything grand or going anywhere special. I learned early to enjoy the simple things in life.

And then there came a time to work and there was always plenty to do. We took turns mowing the yard with the push mower. Your turn consisted of one round then you sat under the tree and waited until it was your turn again. We weeded and hoed the garden and helped with the canning. We would sit in the back yard and break beans or shell peas. I always said, "If we had one person for every bean, it wouldn't take so long to get the job done". Of course, we figured out that if we had that many people it would take a lot more beans to feed them. We took turns ironing shirts and handkerchiefs. We worked together to clean up and wash the dishes after meals. You taught us to sew, cook and clean. We learned how to work, how to work as a team and how good it feels to accomplish tough tasks. I am very grateful for this valuable life skill of a good work ethic.

I learned from you to appreciate the beauty in God's creation… wildflowers, rainbows, dew on a spider web, the beautiful colors of fall. I can't count the times you've called to say, "There's a rainbow! Look out your kitchen window". And sure enough, there would be a beautiful rainbow that we'd enjoy together.

You taught us to develop our minds and always "backed" us in anything we dreamed we could do. You inspired us to be enthusiastic and motivated learners and gave us the desire to always be learning and trying different things. I attribute my successes to your encouragement and you believing in me.

I am extremely blessed to have been born into a family of faith. We were always in church and you taught us how important it is to have a personal relationship with Jesus. This is the most valuable thing you can give to anyone. I am thankful for the daily prayers you send up for your children, grandchildren and great-grandchildren. Gran, Pa and Gay also were daily prayer warriors for all the family members. I am so thankful for these prayers and know for certain it's made a difference in our lives.

These aren't the kind of things that you set out to teach, they just happen because of the person you are. I can now see that the things you value, love and enjoy have become a part of me. Thank you so much for all you have done. I am truly grateful for the influence you have had and continue to have in my life and the lives of my children and grandchildren. I will do my best to see that your influence continues for generations!

FROM SANDRA

I started writing this book because we were doing several projects that we needed lots of help with (bee keeping, gardening, and chickens). Mom is an expert in these areas. I was having to call her continuously to ask her questions about how to do this and that. I had to write it down so I would remember everything, because she is so full of information that when she starts talking about a subject, she gives a lot of information. I had a little book going. So it grew from there. I appreciate Mom for her knowledge.

Mom is not afraid to try new things. (She doesn't like electronics, though.) She isn't afraid to work hard. I am glad that she taught us when we were younger, and that she still teaches us now by her example, how to be hard workers. She often outworks me. This is a lost art today. People have forgotten how to have a good work ethic, how to do a good job, and how to care about what they do. I can still hear a voice saying, "Anything that is worth doing is worth doing right". I redo lots of things that I may not have done well the first time because of that voice that plays in my memory.

That isn't the only saying that comes to me. There are so many that we started to add a chapter of wise sayings to this book. Our Mom is a wise lady. She is full of wisdom and little wise sayings that were passed down to her from her mother. Our mother carries skills and wisdom that represent the generations that come before her. She has been concerned about passing these things down to other generations in our family. There are two generations past ours who have been influenced by this wisdom.

I thank God for our mother. I thank God that we have a mother that we can be proud of. All too often I see children who aren't proud of their parents. I see parents who let their children down because they are too wrapped up in themselves. Mom has never been about herself, from the time when we were small through her life to today. She loves us all. I know that love is the same for all of us. It is still as strong today as it was the day we were born.

Mom, thank you for all you have done, and for all you do now. We all love and appreciate you. You have no idea of all you have done in our lives, and in the lives of your grandchildren, and great grand children. Your great grandchildren and great great grandchildren will be influenced in their lives because of who you are and what you do. On those days when you feel like you haven't accomplished much, just get out this book and read all these tributes. Joyce titled hers, *Tribute to Our Mother*. That is so fitting. These are tributes. And these are thanks. Thank you Mom. I love you.

76735430R00075

Made in the USA
Lexington, KY
21 December 2017